OIL PRICES AND COMPETITION

By Harold Fleming

45377

PRINTED IN THE UNITED STATES

FOREWORD

Few subjects of importance to consumers are as generally misunderstood as oil prices. There seems to be a widespread, but erroneous, belief that in some way oil prices are manipulated through concerted action within the industry.

If this were true, then oil prices have been manipulated for the benefit of the consumer. Gasoline prices, exclusive of Federal and State excise taxes, are no higher today than they were in 1925—and the quality is 50 per cent greater. Crude oil prices, in terms of the purchasing power of the dollar, are at the lowest level in many years.

But oil prices are not manipulated, nor are they set up by anyone or any groups within the petroleum industry. Oil prices are determined, except for periods of government control, by aggressive competition within the framework of supply and demand in a freely functioning market place. They are responsive only to the demands of consumers.

There is no such thing as a formula for determining prices in the American oil industry. Uniform practices are rare. Each seller approaches his problems somewhat differently than do his competitors. Over the years, to be sure, patterns have developed out of the day-to-day operations. But these patterns, in one respect or another, can be, and are, disrupted over-night by vigorous competitors or a change in consumer buying habits.

Accordingly, when the American Petroleum Institute's Oil Industry Information Committee decided that an effort should be made to seek better public understanding of oil prices, it was agreed that facts, not theories, were needed.

To do this job, the committee selected Harold Fleming, well-known for his many years of independent and accurate reporting of current financial and economic developments. His assignment was to find out, at first hand from oil men in all segments of the industry, how petroleum prices are determined—not in theory—but as they are in actual practice.

This volume contains Mr. Fleming's report. His findings and conclusions are his own. We feel that this report will have great value to those interested in pricing of oil and its products. We hope that it will contribute to better public understanding of this complex subject.

Frank M. Porter

President
American Petroleum Institute

March 16, 1953

iii

HOW THIS STUDY WAS WRITTEN

The American Petroleum Institute asked me to do a summary of how oil prices are arrived at. We thought it might run perhaps 5000 words and take perhaps a month.

After two months the first 12,000-word draft was sent out in mimeographed form to companies and firms in the industry for check. Undoubtedly there are a few sentences in this final document which were in the original draft; but I am not sure where they are.

The second draft, of about the same length, went out in November. Gradually, as the comments came in, suggestions for about 150 textual changes took shape. Most were accepted, some rejected. Some were purely factual (such as, "the writer must have meant 3¢ a gallon, not 2¢") while others were on policy (such as, "Suggest this section be thrown out.") I accepted most of them.

The third draft went out around February 15, 1952. It brought in 75 specific suggestions, large and small, from tax, accounting, sales, and law departments. Again, most were accepted, some turned down. (In a few cases different departments of the same company made contradictory suggestions.)

With the changes, a fourth draft went out in August, 1952.

The result embodies the consensus of a host of witnesses in the industry about how oil prices are arrived at. Hundreds of oil men, in all departments of the industry, have had the chance to pass on the drafts of this brochure.

But the story, as here presented, is mine,—an outside writer's view and without change of emphasis. And writers are as independent as oil men (or should be).

I urge on the reader's attention that, unlike many statements about the oil industry, this one has run the gamut of check, double-check, and more, for factual accuracy.

HAROLD FLEMING

March 16, 1953

iv

CONTENTS

OIL PRICES AND COMPETITION

By HAROLD FLEMING

CHAPTER I

INTRODUCTION: — *The Gold-Fish Bowl of Oil Prices*

What determines the prices at which petroleum products are sold? And why is it that gasoline sells at the service station today, pre-tax, no higher than 25 years ago?

Most oil men feel that their industry is one of the country's "fightin'est" as to prices and competition. They feel strongly that, as Supreme Court Justice William O. Douglas recently said, "Today there is vigorous competition between the oil companies for the market." More than that, they feel that there has been such competition in oil for at least forty years—that is, since the old Standard combine was broken up on order of the Supreme Court in 1911.

But oil prices are not easy to understand. No one has ever sat in an ivory tower and had much success in predicting them. For instance price wars continued to break out almost all over the United States, from Los Angeles to the rock-bound shores of Maine, right through the inflationary period of June, 1950, to January, 1951.

As a result some people may have concluded that the oil industry is in a perennial state of cut-throat competition.

Yet other people may have been thinking, in other parts of the country and at the very same time, that there isn't much competition in oil prices after all. Seeing many service stations quoting the same price at the same time, they may have concluded that the dealers had quietly agreed to all charge the same price.

From such contradictory evidence it would be only natural for people to come to contradictory impressions—like the blind men who felt of the elephant. Some might conclude that the industry's competition was too strenuous, others that it was too soft.

This is understandable. The facts about oil prices are of almost infinite variety. They differ from one segment of the industry to another, from state to state, and from company to company. And they keep changing. They involve the varying personalities of thousands of men. They involve, as one student of the industry has put it, "behavior patterns beyond the powers of imagination of even the most fertile-minded theorist."

This may help to explain why the industry's pricing habits have been frequently mis-reported. Where there is so much variety, it is temptingly easy to start with general assumptions and then work down deductively to details and corollaries which sound plausible but often aren't so.

Yet anyone can have all the facts he wants—by digging. They can be found in thousands of pages of legislative hearings. Perhaps no industry has ever had its pricing habits so much investigated. Or he can get the facts from oil men directly. There is no blanket of "security" covering oil prices. The oil industry makes its prices in a gold-fish bowl.

In this booklet we try merely to skim through the top of the story of how competition works and prices are made in oil. The entire story would take many five-foot shelves; in fact it has already filled many of them.

The story starts at the service station, because that is where most people meet the industry.

CHAPTER II

ECONOMICS OF THE RETAIL GASOLINE BUSINESS

A. SERVICE STATION PROBLEMS

SMALL BUSINESS AT WORK

Nineteen out of twenty retail gasoline service stations are operated by dealers in business for themselves. They are self-employed local citizens, operating at their own risk and selling gasoline for their own account. About 200,000 such small business men in the country sell gasoline as their principal line of business. And another 200,000 retail establishments, such as garages, sell gasoline as a sideline.

These dealers decide their own prices. There are no "list prices" in the retail gasoline business. Often the dealer leases the station from the company which built it and whose brand he carries. But he is the one who decides on the price.

"HARD COMPETITION" FOR AN ELUSIVE CUSTOMER

The man who opens a service station lets himself into a very competitive business.

For, in the first place, he handles a nearly uniform product. Usually he handles a widely-known brand which competes with other widely-known brands. But even if he sells a *privately branded* gasoline he is still handling a fairly staple product, insofar as the customer can tell by immediate performance.

In the second place, his customer, the car or truck driver, is extremely choosy. This is because the driver is on wheels. He can be price-conscious or quality-conscious with very little effort. When on foot he might hesitate to walk several blocks for a small saving or gain; but, behind the wheel of a car, he can be elusive and hard to please; distance has become less important to him and his shopping is almost effortless.

Lastly, on the average, this customer does not mind occasionally shifting brands, or even going over to a quite unfamiliar brand—if the price differential looks good enough. Thus, the retail buyer of gasoline is perhaps one of the world's most independent customers.

So the retail gasoline dealer's life is not always an easy one. He must decide—and keep on deciding every day—a number of questions.

UNIT PROFIT VERSUS TOTAL PROFIT

The first of his questions might be called that of "mark-up versus gallonage."

To give an extreme example, he might mark his gasoline up several cents a gallon, and so make considerably more profit *per gallon;* but he would then certainly begin to lose business. Or, conversely, he might mark his gasoline down several cents. He would then certainly gain business; but he wouldn't make much, if anything, *per gallon.*

Thus, one way he might end up with a huge per-gallon profit but no business, and the other way with a huge business but no profit.

The answer he must find is somewhere in between. So he soon learns to look for an *optimum* price, as the economists call it, which will give him largest *total* profit. This is something quite different from *per gallon* profit. It is a product of *mark-up times volume.* This goal will keep him from either "reaching for the sky" or "selling himself down the river."

"ECONOMICS OF OVERHEAD COSTS"

But while he is working on this one, he runs into another question.

Many of his costs, like rent and interest, go on whether he does any business or not. Others, like maintenance, electricity, water and bookkeeping, increase only slowly, he learns, as he increases his business. Also, the more gasoline he sells the better chance he has to sell TBA—the oil man's term for tires, batteries and accessories—at a further profit. Some enterprising dealers figure that on volume increases they can make an additional profit on TBA, oil, grease jobs and other services, of as much as five cents for every added gallon of gasoline sold.

Of course this couldn't go on forever. Somewhere beyond a point, his costs would probably start moving up uncomfortably. But up to there, he has a rather strong incentive, particularly where the traffic is heavy, to bid for more gallonage by inching down his prices. He tries to find that point.

THE "ELASTICITY OF DEMAND" PER STATION

But now he runs into still a third consideration. It is that, since the average customer is so mobile and price-conscious, a small cut in price may bring him a lot more business. Cases have been reported, where the traffic was heavy, of service station operators who jumped their business from 20,000 gallons a month to 100,000 by price-cuts.

Let us see how he might figure. Suppose he is selling 20,000 gallons a month at a mark-up of *five cents a gallon* and he has operating costs of around three cents a gallon. But cutting to a *three-cent mark-up* he might get such an increase in volume, including increased TBA sales, that his per-gallon *cost* might drop to two cents. If then he could *triple* his volume he could make a good deal more money on the smaller mark-up than on the larger. So he might figure somewhat as follows:

	Today	*Imagined*
Mark-up	5 cents	3 cents
Volume in Gallons, monthly	20,000	60,000
Per-gallon Operating Costs	3 cents	2 cents
Per-gallon Profit	**2 cents**	1 cent
Total Profit on Gasoline, monthly	$400.00	$600.00
Estimated Other Profits (TBA), Motor Oil, Service	200.00	600.00
Over-all Profit, monthly	600.00	1,200.00

GOOD-FAITH PRICE COMPETITION

But having figured this out our ambitious dealer has to take another thing into account—or he may receive a severe "come-uppance" from his competitors. Most of the new business he has gained has been at their expense. But they too know the sometimes almost magic effect of price-cuts on station volume. So if he starts cutting, and they start losing business to his station, he can be pretty sure they will start cutting right along with him. And in the end perhaps nobody will make any net gain in gallonage, while everybody will have to take a reduction in mark-up.

Under such circumstances he may reconsider his idea of price-cuts.

Thus, the economics of cutting price to get larger volume and so larger total profit, are not quite so simple as they appear on the surface. Our dealer may find that the level of competitive retail prices eventually turns out to be the result not merely of his own decisions but of the composite reaction of all his competitors in the area—a temporary level arrived at by many minds without consultation or discussion.

SECRET AND NON-PRICE COMPETITION

Meantime, however, he may discover a fifth economic fact of life in the business. He has many other ways of competing for business besides posting a lower competitive price.

For, to begin with, even while all his competitors for some distance around him may be posting the same price, some of them may be quietly offering price-concessions to certain customers, and he can, too.

Also, there are many other forms of competition besides price-competition with which he can lure customers. While still charging the identical price as his competitors, he can bid for more business with better and more courteous service, more attractive rest-rooms and other such non-price inducements.

He may also try to attract customers with offers of premiums, chances on large prizes, and the like. Meantime, his competitors may join the competitive fray with such things as tie-in offers, two-for-one sales, free washing or brake adjustment, cigarettes at a cent a pack, fruit-glasses for the wife, or ice-cream cones or all-day suckers for the kids. All these things have been offered, and many like them.

TRIAL AND ERROR IN PRICE-MAKING

By now our imaginary service station operator has surely latched on to a final basic principle of how to decide on a price. It is that, "You never know 'til you try." No wonder the sales manager of a leading oil company recently said, "The essence of sound pricing is trial and error, a purely grass roots function." He added that his company, which operates a few pilot stations of its own, "carries on experimentation to find the combination of price, volume, services and facilities which will maximize net income."

B. DEALER MARGINS

The national average retail gasoline mark-up or gross margin is around five cents a gallon. Thus on a national average, if the price at the pump is around 27 cents, or around 20 cents before state and federal taxes, the dealer probably averaged to pay a tank-wagon price of around 15 cents.

This average gross margin has increased in recent years—in cents per gallon, though not necessarily in percentage of the tank-wagon price. In the period, 1935-1939, it averaged around 3.90 cents. But while this increase of around 30 per cent in the *mark-up per gallon* is somewhat less than the increase in the cost of living, the average dealer's *total income* has increased considerably more than this, for the average station volume is much larger. Average dollar sales per service station were $11,670 in 1939, and $34,439 in 1948, according to the government's 1948 census of business (as reported in the National Petroleum News of September 5, 1951.) Thus the dealer who merely holds his competitive position in the business has an almost steady "normal" increase in volume on which to make more *total income*.

On the other hand, of course, dealer operating costs also have risen at the same time, notably for wages and equipment.

C. SUPPLIER OPERATIONS

VARIED OUTLETS

When a customer sees a supplying company's brand-name hanging in front of a service station, it seldom means that the company itself operates the station.

Actually there are at least four different ways in which the gasoline may have moved from the brand-name supplier to the customer. They are as follows:

> 1. He may in very rare cases be buying directly from the company itself in a company-operated station. A few brand-name companies operate stations of their own; some operate none at all except as "pilot stations" for experiments in pricing or as training stations for dealers. Some nationally or almost nationally known companies who

distribute through thousands of stations actually operate only a score or two.

2. He may be buying from a dealer who bought direct from the company that puts out the brand.

3. He may be buying gasoline that has been sold by the company to a jobber or wholesaler who in turn has sold and delivered it to the dealer who runs the station.

4. He may be buying from a jobber-operated station.

Perhaps the best way to show this is by the following chart:

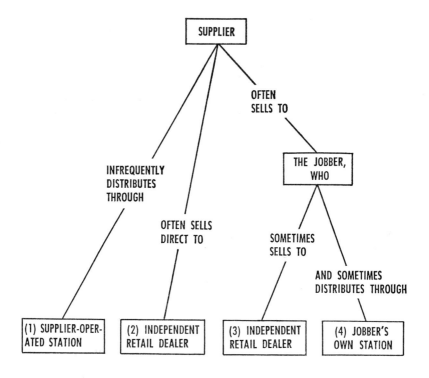

SUPPLIER-DEALER RELATIONS

The relations between the dealer who carries a branded gasoline and the company which regularly supplies him are necessarily close.

The dealer wants to do business with a company which will deal with him fairly, keep him supplied with a good brand of gasoline, back him up with advertising and promotion and, perhaps, give him some help in case of a price war.

On the other hand, the company wants to do business with a dealer who is capable, solvent and ambitious to sell a large volume of the company's gasoline and related products.

And they must both keep in good competitive position to meet the normal strenuous competition of the business and the occasional price war. So they have to work together.

SUPPLIER-JOBBER RELATIONS

The big suppliers of well-known brand-names share no uniform policies as to distributing through jobbers or distributing directly to the retail service station operator. One well-known company sells entirely through jobbers and never direct to retail dealers. Another well-known company sells all its products directly to retail dealers and none to jobbers. Still other companies sell in some areas only to jobbers and in other areas only to retailers. And lastly some companies even sell in the same area to both jobbers and retailers.

Adding to the almost infinite diversity of the sales channels through which the oil industry distributes, some companies sell a part of their product through varying types of bulk-plant commission operators, some of whom are entirely independent of company control and some of whom are not, depending upon the particular contractual arrangement between the supplier and the bulk-plant operator.

Selling in the same area both direct to retailers and to jobbers, who in turn sell to retailers, is called *dual distribution*. Many companies are giving it up. Some explain that under *dual distribution* they cannot adequately plan their own sales programs; others say that they thus find they are competing against themselves. So they are moving toward putting their different sales areas on either all-direct or all-jobber distribution.

Some jobbers of well-known gasoline brands operate on such a large scale that they also face the same problem of *dual distribution,* and also answer it in varying ways.

15

The relations between jobbers and suppliers of brand-name gasoline are in some respects the most successful and in some respects the most touchy in the industry.

To some extent the brand-name jobber is the grass-roots, unsung and insufficiently honored rugged individualist of the oil industry, since he buys and sells at his own risk, yet is seldom known to the driving public by his own business name, but only by the brand-name of the gasoline he handles.

COMPETITION BETWEEN BRAND-NAME SUPPLIERS

In every state of the Union there are at least a half-dozen suppliers of widely-known gasoline brands competing. In some states there are as many as fifteen. For all states there are on the average nine such suppliers competing on the basis of price, quality and service.

Nor with this is the story complete. Some smaller companies, not important on a country-wide basis, are very important in smaller areas and do a large part of the local business. In every locality buyers of gasoline have a free choice of many brands.

D. UNBRANDED GASOLINES

One of the things that makes for "seldom a dull moment" in the gasoline business is the so-called *unbranded gasoline*. Often it is some-one who offers this gasoline at a discount who starts a price war.

Unbranded gasoline cannot be defined exactly. It has many grada-tions. Some is totally orphan gasoline "without pride of paternity or hope of posterity." Some is sold on specifications which are as high as those of some widely-known brands.

By the time such gasoline reaches the service station pump it, of course, has been given a brand, which will eventually acquire as good or as poor a name as it deserves. But even then it is often still called, in the trade, *unbranded gasoline*.

However, there is no precise definition of the word *unbranded*. Often little-known brands are called *private brands*. There are locally-known *private brands,* regionally-known brands, widely-known brands and two or three nationally-known brands. *Private brands* may vary in quality from mediocre to as good as a driver can find anywhere.

16

Unbranded gasoline has many sources. It may come from brand-name refiners who have temporarily produced more than they can market through their regular sources under their regular brand name. And some refiners make a gasoline of lower quality than house brand, which they regularly sell at a lower price to reflect the difference in quality. Or it may come from independent refiners.

Little-known brands of gasoline usually sell at a discount, which ranges from 1 cent to as much as 4 cents below the price of widely-known brands. This is often due to the *unbranded* seller's belief that he must offer an inducement to offset the public's natural inclination to buy a product it knows more about or to offset differences in services provided the motorist.

E. PRICE WARS

Gasoline price wars sometimes seem to spread like forest fires. The ease with which these price wars often spread shows how fragile is the camouflage of identical prices which sometimes obscures a state of cold competition about to break out into a hot price war.

These wars start in many ways and from many sources. They may for instance be begun by operators working with such new merchandising ideas as multi-pumps, with as many as 24 pumps to a station, or with the new *self-serve* and *semi-serve* methods. Outsiders often try to enter the business with new selling techniques, or established dealers decide to try the dangerous but exciting gamble of bidding for larger volume with price cuts. Or dealers offering premiums and prizes may change the situation.

Another common starter of price wars is *unbranded* or *locally branded* gasoline. An operator selling such gasoline in large volume undercuts going prices and the whole price structure starts coming down all around him.

The move may result from several factors, such as economy of merchandising, or lower costs. Anyway, it usually involves an attempt to increase volume.

Thus, for instance, price wars have started when some enterprising distributor decided to by-pass a bulk plant and serve retail service

17

stations direct from a refinery or harbor or river terminal. This change of channel of distribution has been going on for a number of years and still continues.

On the other hand, some oil men feel that the most frequent fundamental cause of price wars is a surplus of gasoline in the wholesale market.

In any case, price wars tend to spread like ripples when a stone is thrown into the water. Frequently their influence will spread over an area with a radius of 100 miles in any direction. It has been said, perhaps with some exaggeration, that one operator in the middle of New England pulled down the region's prices as far away as Boston, Rhode Island and Connecticut.

SUPPLIERS IN PRICE WARS

When price wars break out among dealers, brand-name suppliers are usually drawn in sooner or later.

All major suppliers are, of course, interested in having strong retail dealer outlets. And so, if their dealers get caught in a price war, it is to their interest to come to their rescue and help them survive. No supplier will abandon his dealers to competition without a fight.

Suppliers back their dealers during price wars in varying ways. The most obvious, of course, is to give the dealer a lower tank-wagon price, but suppliers sometimes do it in other ways less direct sometimes called *voluntary allowances* or even *subsidies*.

Suppliers differ in how far and how widely they will share their dealers' price-war difficulties. For price-cutting can easily spread from a city to a county and from there up and down a main highway. If local dealers get help, the next outer circle of dealers want it too, and then the next. This presents difficulties. Supplying companies have to bear in mind the prohibitions in the Clayton and Robinson-Patman Act against discrimination between one customer (dealer) and another one next door or a mile down the highway but in the same *trading area*. And the definition of *trading area* "depends on what law department you consult."

18

Price wars always come to an end; but only in the sense that it always stops raining. The retail gasoline price structure is always subject to "change without notice," due to changes in the methods of station operation, in consumer preferences, in the general economic situation, in the underlying petroleum price structure, and so on.

One of the results of price wars is a rather painful one for some competitors but a helpful one for consumers. Such wars apply in a rather harsh way the so-called "law of the survival of the fittest." The "fittest," in such cases, are the dealers and suppliers with the lowest costs. It is they who come out of such wars least hurt.

F. ARTIFICIAL PRICE RESTRAINTS

Occasionally someone—usually through organizations of dealers—tries to keep up the price of gasoline or the per-gallon margin on it by artificial means—which is to say, with the support of law.

Such efforts are ordinarily made during or just after price wars. This is natural. Price wars hurt. It is understandable that some dealers should try to ward off *hard competition* by laws.

The basis for most such efforts is the *unfair sales law* on the statute books of about three-fourths of the states. These laws, in general, make it illegal to charge less for a thing than cost; in many states, the minimum mark-up is specified, ranging from one to 12 per cent in different states.

In some states the law has been further elaborated so that a local dealer's organization can hire a certified public accountant who will attest to the average or median cost of selling gasoline in that area. Thereafter any dealer selling at a mark-up which is less than this estimated cost can be haled into court; and unless he has good books to prove a below-average unit cost he can find himself in legal trouble.

Indirect methods are sometimes used. A dealer's association may recommend certain selling prices or certain minimum mark-ups. Such methods however may run afoul of state or federal antitrust laws, as has happened in Wisconsin (state law) and Connecticut (federal law).

But even when such efforts will stand up legally, some old heads in the oil industry say that they will not stand up economically. They say they are bound to end in eventual failure.

G. RETAIL GASOLINE BUSINESS TYPICAL OF AMERICAN BUSINESS

The retail gasoline business typifies the most strenuously competitive aspects of American business in general.

All the considerations mentioned above in retail gasoline selling are also considerations of American business in general. These considerations are:

1. The most profit does not come from the highest price.

2. Unit costs tend to decrease with greater volume.

3. Small price cuts may bring large volume increases for individual stations.

4. Prices are usually the result of the composite reaction of competitors.

5. There are many other forms of competition besides price-competition.

6. The essence of sound pricing is trial and error.

The first three of these have been considerations of typical successful American businesses for generations. They have chosen smaller per-unit profits as the best way, via larger volume, toward larger total profits.

This was, for instance, the method of Henry Ford when the FORD MOTOR COMPANY, almost 40 years ago, announced it would produce a car for the common man at $500 and a job for the common man at $5.00 a day. This reach for volume rather than high price also made for the growth of the radio business and more recently of the television business. The airlines have grown by it and tried it recently in their so-called coach fares. The policy of low mark-ups to get larger volume, and profits, was pioneered in the grocery business by THE GREAT ATLANTIC & PACIFIC TEA COMPANY. It has long been a policy of the electric power companies. In fact, it has been the normal method by which American industry has grown and American living standards have been raised.

And the reach for volume through lower prices has been a historic characteristic of the oil industry, not only in marketing but clear back to crude oil production. The whole industry has grown by mass production and repeatedly lowered costs.

Thus the established retail gasoline dealer, from his personal experience of the inter-relations between mark-up, volume, and total profit, may often be far better equipped than most people to understand how the profit system actually works. Few people have as much experience as he in the ways by which free competition tends to encourage the man who reaches for larger volume and lower unit costs over the man who looks merely to higher prices and larger mark-ups for his living.

In fact, the retail gasoline business, as practiced daily on every highway and at every cross-road in America, offers an excellent field for study by economists and students of marketing. A really hard look at this highly American and highly competitive business might dispel some of the conclusions drawn deductively about the oil industry from such cloudy abstract concepts as *monopolistic competition* and *oligopoly.*

CHAPTER III

THE WHOLESALE GASOLINE MARKET

Some people say that competition in the wholesaling of oil products is even more strenuous than in the retail end. True, the people who say this are mostly wholesalers.

There is a wholesale gasoline price *structure* all over the United States. This is another way of saying that wholesale gasoline prices everywhere are related to wholesale gasoline prices almost everywhere else in the country. There are measurable reasons why gasoline costs more in some places, less in others.

A. GEOGRAPHICAL ADJUSTMENTS

Most crude oil is produced in the southwestern part of the country. But most of it, in product form, is consumed in the central and eastern areas. So it has to travel.

The Atlantic seaboard's oil products come chiefly by water from the Gulf of Mexico, particularly from the Texas Gulf Coast.

The Chicago and Great Lakes consuming areas, on the other hand, have a number of alternate sources of supply, such as Louisiana, Oklahoma, Kansas and even Illinois, Ohio, Pennsylvania, Michigan, Indiana, and Kentucky.

Wholesale prices generally tend to vary in relation to each other according to the resulting differences in transportation costs. The relation is not precise. Competition, affected by local changes in supply or demand or both, may bring about relationships for a time which are out of keeping with transport costs. Local marketing costs differ among areas.

Over the long run, however, geographic price variations tend to fit around variations in costs of transport. This applies as much to the complicated West Coast market as to the East.

These variations are much like those between prices of wheat in such different markets as Chicago, Minneapolis, Kansas City and New

York, or of cotton in such different markets as Hattiesburg, Mississippi; New Orleans; New York; or New Bedford, Massachusetts.

TRANSPORT COSTS

But these normal variations in price between areas are not measurable simply by distances as the crow flies. They are determined largely by transport costs.

Thus for instance it is a good deal further to the Appalachians from the Gulf Coast via the East Coast than it is from Kansas or Illinois—in miles. But most of the distance from the Gulf Coast is by ocean tanker. And ocean tanker costs per mile are less than pipeline costs, while pipeline costs per mile are less than the cost of railway tank car movement.

Sometimes prices along some major transport line will show clearly the effect of the cost of moving the gasoline. Near the start of the line the prices will be the lowest; near the end, the highest.

> For instance, there is a heavy barge-movement of gasoline up the Mississippi. Of course, the barge-captain first stops at New Orleans, then Memphis, then St. Louis, then Twin Cities. The further up the river, the higher the cost, it might be asssumed. The figures bear this out. For the three years, 1948-1950, the average prices of gasoline delivered to stations in these cities were: New Orleans, 13.19¢; Memphis, 14.93¢; St. Louis, 15.39¢; and Twin Cities, 15.89¢.

> For another example, the cost of tanker and product pipeline movement from the Gulf of Mexico east and north is reflected in the following average prices: New Orleans, 13.19¢; Charleston, 13.51¢; New York, 13.82¢; Buffalo, 14.49¢. (These quotations of course do not include tax, which applies at the point of retail sale.)

But differences in transport cost have for decades been in a constant state of flux. Someone is always finding new ways to lower transport costs and so to foil mere geography. Crude oil pipe lines were the first of such methods. But in recent years the geographical cost-structure has been upset and revised by such developments as (1) increased river-barge movements and more efficient tows; (2) construction of product pipe lines; (3) increased highway movement by transport truck; and (4) use of giant tankers carrying as much as 200,000 barrels at higher speeds and lower costs per barrel per mile.

B. WHO ADJUSTS THESE PRICES TO EACH OTHER?

The constantly changing geographical variations in the wholesale price of gasoline are not automatic. They do not result merely from cost differences. They are the result of the composite reaction of a great many skilled buyers and sellers who either know these cost differentials or learn their results from competitive conflicts with other buyers and sellers.

> Some people might think that a single agency, group, board, clique, or individual, acting as a *central brain,* could dictate these variations. No such brain, brain trust, or trust, exists in fact or could do the job in theory. "It takes everybody to know everything" even about this partial segment of the oil business. Such a *centralized brain* would soon get as mixed up in its decisions as the fabled self-conscious centipede.

THE "TELEPHONE MARKET"

The wholesale market for gasoline is not quite like the market for wheat, cotton, or corn, with brokers throwing bids and offers at each other around a pit. It is more like the *telephone market* in unlisted securities or in government bonds. But it is highly sensitive from hour to hour to all kinds of influences and moods in different parts of the country. An amazing variety of people have a hand in the making of these prices. And there are hundreds, and sometimes thousands, of both sellers and buyers.

To begin with there are over 200 companies owning about 350 refineries with gasoline for sale at one time or another.

Some of these refineries have no operations in other branches of the industry. Others are owned by integrated or semi-integrated companies. Some of these companies, with noted brand-names, consistently refine more gasoline than they distribute under the brand-name, and so always have gasoline to sell; while others just as consistently distribute more than they refine, and therefore always have gasoline needs to fill.

Lastly and most importantly, a great many refiners always sell their entire output, and a great many wholesalers and jobbers, including some very large companies indeed, have no refineries at all and buy their entire requirements either on contract or in the open market.

24

In general three kinds of buyers compete for wholesale gasoline. They are the integrated oil company's wholesale buyer; the gasoline jobber or wholesaler; and last but not least, the gasoline broker. In addition, some consumers like the federal government and large bus and trucking fleets buy gasoline directly in bulk.

CASE OF THE BUFFALO JOBBER

An instance of how oil-product prices are kept in adjustment may be the following:

> A jobber in Number Two fuel oil (home-heating oil) in Buffalo, New York, has a local market for 50,000 gallons at the moment at a price. He wants to know whether he can fill the order at a profit. He does not always depend on a single supplier, nor count on a single market, nor wait on the telegraph or airmail. To find out what the market is he first studies the trade paper price lists, then telephones first New York, then Cleveland, then Chicago, then perhaps Tulsa, and then compares the prices he gets against the costs he would incur to get the product to Buffalo by product pipe line, barge, lake transportation or tank car. If he could bring it in cheaper on horseback he would do so.

INFLUENCE OF THE "SPOT MARKET"

The gasoline market is somewhat like the *marriage market*. A large part of the business is tied up on long-term contract. But there inevitably remains a *spot market* like the Lonely Hearts Club, where business is done between buyers seeking sellers and sellers seeking buyers. This is the so-called *non-contractual market*.

While this *non-contractual* or *spot market* does only a small proportion of the business, the prices made here have a large influence on prices made on long-term contract. In a sense its influence seems all out of proportion to its size, like the tail wagging the dog. Yet in another sense this is quite understandable. It is like the fact that the day-to-day prices of common stocks such as U. S. STEEL or GENERAL MOTORS on the Stock Exchange are made by the purchase and sale of only a few thousand shares while the total of outstanding shares runs in the millions. It is here that supply and demand are brought into balance by a multitude of independent day-to-day price adjustments.

Hence oil men often say that in the last analysis *the* wholesale price for gasoline is often led by the small, independent, or marginal refiner and works out through the "law of supply and demand." In a weak market it is this independent refiner's distress gasoline, sold through the broker, which sets off a decline, and in a tight market it is the higher price which he can and does ask which starts the rise. Though only a small proportion of the total business is done in this way, the resulting prices have a very large influence on contract prices.

BROKERS

The broker is the hub of substantial sales in the *spot market*. He neither works on a payroll nor has one; but he knows where gasoline is to be had, who wants it, and what the going prices are in various places and by various buyers and sellers.

The broker more often than not deals in *unbranded gasoline*. For obvious reasons, very little branded gasoline finds its way into the open market; when it does, it usually loses its brand. If, for instance, an integrated refiner-marketer company finds extra gasoline on its hands, it may offer this to a broker; if, on the other hand, it finds itself short, it may ask a broker to locate some extra gasoline or refining capacity.

In the former case the gasoline sold will lose its brand; in the latter case the buying company will provide the unknown seller, through the broker, with its specifications; and the unknown gasoline will eventually appear with a new name.

But if the homeless gasoline finds a home with a terminal operator, or a small jobber, or a large service station operator, it will eventually have to appear at the final retail gasoline-pump as *unbranded* or *privately branded* gasoline.

TANK-WAGON PRICES

But while these spot or non-contractual prices are especially sensitive to influences from the refinery or supply end of the business, another designation of prices is closer related to the retail or consumer-demand end. This includes the *tank-wagon price* and its usual corollary, the *tank-car price*.

Competing methods long ago blurred the original meaning of these terms. But the *tank-wagon price* is still the established price of gasoline as delivered, originally by wagon, to the service station. It is, next to the price at the pump itself, the grassroots price in the business, sensitive to all the influences which affect the ultimate consumer.

Next before it, the *tank-car price* was originally, as the name indicates, the price in tank-car (that is, much larger) lots. Today the *tank-car price* is usually the contractual price made by suppliers to jobbers or wholesalers, regardless of whether the gasoline comes by rail, barge, pipeline or tanker.

The history of how different suppliers have figured their tank-wagon prices is a long one. Brand-name supplying companies have been wrestling with the problem of how to figure their *tank-wagon prices* ever since there have been service stations; and they will probably continue wrestling with it as long as there are suppliers, jobbers and dealers.

The first and simplest method was to take the wholesale price at the nearest refinery center, add the transportation cost to the bulk plant, and then add the cost of getting the gasoline from there to the dealer.

This soon proved all too simple. Some competitors appeared with gasoline from new refineries in new areas, and others appeared with gasoline brought by new methods over new routes. *Track-side operators* (getting deliveries direct to service stations by railroad tank-cars) and then newcomers with big trucks began to by-pass conventional bulk-plant distribution methods. By the 'thirties and 'forties the competitive free-for-all in *tank-wagon prices* reminded old-line market men of Lewis Carroll's "and thick and fast they came at last. And more, and more, and more—."

Successful marketers revised their pricing policies. They gave less weight to costs and more and more weight to competitive market factors.

In general, brand-name suppliers keep the following principles in mind in making *tank-wagon prices;* and since these principles sometimes do not lead to the same price-conclusions, they try to hit on some compromise among them.

> 1. In the long run, the price must cover costs; but in the short run, it must meet competition. Costs set a floor on prices, and competition a ceiling.

> 2. The company wants to stay in business for many years, and it has to have outlets.

27

3. But the company is not in business for love, and cannot indefinitely sell at prices which are below costs.

4. The company cannot afford to take advantage of every temporary surge of demand or shortage of supply to get every penny of higher price possible.

5. But on the other hand the company cannot afford to meet every competitive price cut, unless it and the dealers who handle its brand begin to lose business seriously.

6. The making of prices is not a science, but a day-to-day art, dependent, basically, on judgment. The marketing department must take into account such present factors as the wholesale market, the retail demand, and industry inventory, and such future prospects as weather, economic trends, and what news it gets of competitors' policies.

TANK-CAR PRICES

Tank-wagon prices have a powerful influence on *tank-car* prices. They usually move up and down fairly closely. The supplier's *tank-car* price to the jobber generally reflects what the supplier feels is a reasonable margin under the prevailing *tank-wagon* price.

In dealing with the jobbers of its products, a company supplying branded gasoline must, like the elephant, be careful where it sets its feet among its smaller friends. The jobber's existence often depends on the margin between the *tank-car* price which the supplier charges him, and the *tank-wagon* price which he in turn charges to retailers. The company particularly which has a dual distribution system in the same area must pay continuous attention to the margin between these two prices as well as to the other factors set forth above and below.

But this brings us back, via the *tank-car* price, to the general wholesale market. For *tank-car* prices involve and influence the contractual prices which make up the bulk of this market.

INFLUENCES FROM ALL DIRECTIONS

Thus in the wholesale market there are all sorts of influences, combining at all times, in different proportions. They include the interplay on each other of spot prices and contractual prices, of prices for branded and for unbranded gasolines, and of refinery conditions and retail conditions.

It would be well-nigh impossible to measure at any time the specific weight of each, or to chart precisely the channels through which influence is most directly felt. Buyers and sellers must have wide contacts, quick wits, and good judgment; the market is always in flux, responding in various degrees to various forces.

This is why, as stated above, the wholesale gasoline market is "highly sensitive from hour to hour to all kinds of influences and moods in different parts of the country" and of the business.

WHY NO TRADING PIT ?

Some people have asked why the oil industry has not developed a trading pit, or auction market, where brokers can call out their bids and offers as is done with many basic commodities. There are several reasons. One is that oil products are extremely expensive to store and can be handled most economically only if they are kept moving; the chief reason why any of them are stored is merely to make sure of a constant flow to meet sharp fluctuations in demand. Oil is one commodity that is seldom held on speculation, except in the sense that jobbers' buying or not buying to meet anticipated winter requirements assumes aspects of speculation.

PUBLISHED QUOTATIONS

A wide variety of petroleum prices are quoted daily in a number of publications. These usually give high, low and sometimes intermediate quotations.

The oldest of these devoted exclusively to petroleum prices is PLATT'S OILGRAM PRICE SERVICE. Professional oil reporters in half a dozen leading oil markets contact hundreds of primary suppliers (refiners and tanker terminal operators) and an even larger number of other sources such as jobbers, compounders, large consumers, distributors, brokers, tank-car marketers, and so on, for prices at regular intervals.

Other publications which print oil prices regularly include THE OIL DAILY, the NEW YORK JOURNAL OF COMMERCE, and the WALL STREET JOURNAL.

CHAPTER IV

THE ECONOMICS OF REFINING

The man who runs a refinery, be he working for someone else or running his own plant, has to constantly adjust and readjust his refinery operations to the prices which his various finished products bring, as well as the demand for the products. If he doesn't, he won't stay in business long.

This adjustment, however, is far from a simple one. The economic facts of life in refinery operations are complicated, like refining itself. Following are some of the reasons why such adjustment takes thought.

A. CONTINUOUS OPERATIONS AND "DISTRESS GASOLINE"

A refinery runs continuously 24-hours a day, seven days a week. This permits the refiner to spread his heavy overhead costs over the maximum amount of products because the plants are used around the clock. Petroleum refining is a mass production industry.

However, a refinery manager cannot always count on a continuous market for all he can produce—at least at a price which is profitable. While in all branches of the petroleum industry there is a premium on large-scale, continuous and steady movement, consumer demand is not so steady and its fluctuations back up, so to speak, through the wholesale market to the refinery gate.

Neither is the supply constant; someone is always building a competing new refinery somewhere and putting it *on stream,* or developing a new transport method which puts some competitor nearer a market, nearer a source of supply, or otherwise in a more favorable competitive position.

Thus, the refiner is in the position of grandma on the farm, who never knew till sundown how many cousins were coming to supper. He always, to some extent, faces the problem of adjusting his continuous supply to a fickle demand. Temporary over-production can happen to any refiner, whether he is an independent or a part of an integrated company.

When demand for a refiner's products shrinks, the shrinkage does not appear to him first in the form of a statistic, a news story, or a government statement. It first shows on the video screen of his daily life in the form of fuller and fuller storage tanks and in lower prices bid for his products. And incidentally his customers are even more mobile than those of the retail service station operator. While the car-owner has only to drive on to the next service station to see if he can get a better price, the wholesale buyer of gasoline or heating oil has only to pick up the phone and in half an hour he can shop all over the United States.

At this point many a refiner may have wished he was running some kind of operation like a factory which, during a temporary lull in demand, can be kept going and its products piled in the warehouse. But the cost of storage in the oil business is extremely high. The refiner can afford to run only a few days' or weeks' supply into tanks.

So, with prices running against him, our typical refiner's first impulse, be he independent or integrated, might be to shut down the plant. For if he merely decreases his rate of *through-put,* he knows he will soon find himself turning out products at higher cost to sell for a lower price. So he might say to himself, "There is no use in turning out products for which the market will pay only $50,000 a day which my accountants tell me are costing $55,000 to produce."

But here he faces another economic fact of life in his business. It may be more economical to keep running and lose a little money every day than to shut and lose a good deal more per day.

Many costs continue whether a refinery is running or not, including both the out-of-pocket costs of maintenance and administrative staffs, and the bookkeeping costs of interest and depreciation on the heavy investment. It may prove cheaper to lose $5,000 a day while operating than to lose twice that much a day by shutting down.

In fact the seeming paradox may go even further. It may even seem worth while to our refinery manager—if he thinks the drop in prices is purely temporary—to keep running even with prospective prices so low that he would lose more with his plant running than with it closed. For it costs a good deal to shut down and a good deal more to start up.

31

And he may have still one more reason for continuing to run at a loss, especially if he is with an integrated company. If he shuts down, the unhappy effect of the stoppage may go all the way back to the oil fields. If he doesn't take his customary amount of crude oil, that much less can be produced. But even in the oil field many overhead costs continue whether the oil is flowing or not.

Also, if the refiner stops buying crude, he may "lose his connections." Somebody else may start buying it, and when he wants to resume the connection he may not be able to.

In short, the answer in a falling market to the refiner's question, "To run, or not to run?" is to do "whichever would mean the *least loss."*

So the refiner's best bet may often be to keep running even at very low prices and, since he cannot store it indefinitely, to offer his surplus on the market for what he can get. The resulting so-called *distress cargoes* of spot gasoline, offered through brokers, often have a strong depressing effect on prices.

Of course, there is eventually a point in a declining market below which it becomes economical to close a refinery down. This is because refineries vary widely in comparative efficiency, some being high-cost and some low-cost. New refineries are constantly being built which, with improved techniques, can produce the same quality products at lower costs, or better quality products at the same costs. As these come *on stream,* they can afford to take the market away from, or undersell, the older, higher-cost refineries or in other words to sell at prices so low that the higher-cost refineries must shut down.

This is one of the important ways in which the supply of petroleum products is normally adjusted to the demand. It works through price on the marginal refinery. When demand falls, prices fall, and when prices fall, supply falls.

B. "JOINT PRODUCTS"

Refiners convert a barrel of oil into a variety of *joint products.* These range from the highest-test gasolines down through the middle dis-

32

tillates (like kerosine and home-heating oils) to the residuals or left-overs like bunker fuel oil. Thus, refiners are somewhat like meat-packers who convert a steer into a variety of products ranging in value from sirloin steak down to glue.

But the refiner has a more flexible operation than the meat-packer. By working over his products enough, at additional cost of course, he can *up-grade* his final products almost indefinitely. Some oil men go so far as to say that the modern refinery could make 100 per cent gasoline of certain crudes if it so decided. But no refiner would do this unless gasoline sold at such a very large differential over all other products as to justify the very large cost of such re-working.

In practice the refiner watches the current price spreads between the different products he can make and adjusts his operations according-ingly. If these spreads favor the more expensive products by enough to justify it, he will spend the money to rework more of his lower valued products into more valuable ones. But if the spread should narrow again, he will not feel that this *up-grading* pays any more, and will revert to putting out a larger quantity of lower quality products. Thus the market differentials or price spreads between gasoline, mid-dle distillates and residuals are his constant concern, and determine to a considerable degree how much of each he makes.

This helps level out or stabilize the prices of petroleum products. For instance, if gasoline sells at four cents a gallon over heating oils, there will be more gasoline produced and less heating oils; but if this market spread is narrowed by a drop in gasoline prices or a rise in heating oil prices, there will be less gasoline produced and more heat-ing oils.

It may astonish the layman that refiners cannot give any exact figure on the per-gallon cost of producing any particular refinery product such as gasoline, but only a hypothetical or statistical cost figure based on an arbitrarily chosen through-put. The accounting cost of each refinery product depends on the prices at which the others are sold.

Thus, for instance, the refiner may have to sell his residuals at less per barrel than the cost of the crude oil from which he makes them. Should he then charge this loss to the cost of making gasoline, or divide it among the costs of all his non-residual products, and if the latter, in what proportion? Refiners make elaborate hypothetical cost estimates on their different products, but these have meaning only in terms of the hypothesis on which they are based.

In a multiple-product industry like this, cost accountants consider it impossible to find individual product costs with acceptable accuracy. They can make only highly arbitrary allocations of how such general costs as raw material, overhead, financing, maintenance and processing shall be allocated to the several products. They have to make these allocations only because, for income tax and inventory pricing purposes, there has to be some acceptable agreed-on method of figuring product costs.

C. THE POST-WAR "OCTANE RACE"

Since World War II, the oil industry has spent over $2,000,000,000 in refineries, in such structures as new *cat crackers* and other giant new equipment for the *re-forming* of the grosser hydrocarbon molecules into the daintier molecules such as go into high-octane gasoline.

One result has of course been a large increase in the industry's total refining capacity. Also there has been a sharp increase in the industry's capacity to produce quality products. In fact the distinction between the two increases—in quantity and in quality of output, is not always sharp. To some extent they are interchangeable. Much of the new equipment can be used either to *up-grade* the quality of products at a lower rate of output, or to increase the rate of output, but of lower-quality products. This is much as though a dairy business were expanded so that it could turn out either more milk of the same richness or the same amount of milk but richer. Some refiners now use a term, *the octane barrel,* which includes the factors of both quality and quantity.

The quality competition has appeared in the so-called *octane race* in which refiners have supplied, between 1946 and 1951, steadily better gasolines at an average increase of about one octane rating point per year. The same was true for many years before the War.

To put it another way, the two billions competitively invested in pipes, towers, compressors and so on, have enabled refiners not only to handle more crude oil but to get out of each barrel better gasolines and more light products, and have less residuals left.

Refiners' gross margins total—on a very rough average—only about 2½ cents a gallon, or about a dollar a barrel. Since World War II the national average has fluctuated between about 80 cents and $1.10 per barrel. This is the spread between what they pay for their crude oil and what they get for their products.

Perhaps, on the average, 20 cents of this represents the cost of bringing the crude oil from the well to the refinery. However, though this might be everybody's average, it is hardly anybody's actual figure. Some refineries sit right over an oil field, while others, located nearer the consumer, may bring their crude oil as much as 2,000 miles.

Out of the balance of this spread or gross margin, the refiner must pay his manufacturing costs, expects to recover his depreciation, and hopes to make a profit.

But this 2-2½ cents a gallon is only an average. Technological progress is so fast in petroleum refining, particularly in the *octane race,* that while new refineries coming *on stream* with the newest techniques make more than this, older refineries which were once themselves the latest thing can hardly make ends meet. Like Alice and the Red Queen in "Through the Looking Glass," the company that wants to stay in the competitive race has to run hard, in the sense of keeping up with technological developments, to stay in the same competitive place. In oil refining, continuous and successful innovation, at ever increasing capital cost, is the only way to stay in business.

CHAPTER V

CRUDE OIL PRICES

A. THE "POSTED PRICE"

Crude oil is bought in the oil fields at the *posted price*. A buyer *posts* a price at which he will take all the oil offered by anybody in that field who can produce it legally.

Anyone—corporation or individual, refiner or speculator—is free to go into a field and *post* any price he feels like.

But most of the time everybody *posts* the same price, or in other words, in any given field there is usually only one *posted price*. The reason is fairly obvious. If there are two *posted prices,* as sometimes happens, the buyer posting the higher price gets all the oil. Thus, any would-be buyer can pay the highest *posted price* or stay out of the field and get his oil somewhere else. He is in a position somewhat like that of the bidder at an auction; he is free to either meet other buyers' bids or quit bidding.

There are usually more sellers than buyers of crude oil in the oil fields. This is because there are literally thousands of oil men who drill and find oil, while the number of refiners, for obvious reasons, is in the hundreds. Most of the major or integrated companies are consistently in the market for crude oil, since these companies almost invariably refine more than they produce. On the other hand, most companies and individuals who find and produce oil would rather not get into the complications of refining—or can't afford it.

This is not significant for the price of crude oil. It does not mean that the single buyer has a monopoly—since other buyers are always free to enter. If he doesn't offer enough, other buyers will come in, since "enough" means a price based on the market for petroleum products, less refining costs, and less transportation costs. Crude oil prices are determined in the last analysis by nation-wide and world-wide factors of supply and demand for finished and delivered petroleum products.

Crude oil prices vary from field to field according to such considerations as location, gravity, and quality. Oil near tidewater, for instance, is naturally worth more than oil in remote mountain areas. Many a producer in a new field has sold his oil for a dollar or so a barrel to anyone who would truck it away, but obtained a higher price promptly and naturally when a pipe line to a larger market came in. Likewise high-gravity oil with a high potential gasoline content is worth more than low-gravity oil good chiefly for fuel oil. For similar reasons sweet oil is worth more than oil with a high sulphur content. And crude oil which yields a higher percentage of lubricants has always commanded premium prices. Buyers and sellers take all these things into account.

B. CHANGES IN THE POSTED PRICE

Upward movements in the price of crude oil are typified in what has happened since World War II.

The price of crude oil was held unchanged in all major fields throughout the war by government action, with the cooperation of the oil industry. At the same time, civilian and industrial demand was greatly restricted by rationing. At the end of the war, the average price of crude oil at wells in the United States was $1.22.

As rationing ended and demand increased, the first effect appeared in the oil fields in the form of premiums being paid over the *posted price*. These soon became widespread. Very shortly the companies who persisted in buying merely at the *posted price* began to "lose connections." Somebody else was getting the oil. The *posted price* rapidly lost meaning. Finally the low-price buyers, to keep on getting the oil they needed for the increased demand, had to raise their *posted prices* to a more realistic level. Only then did the makeshift premium system disappear.

This happened several times, until the typical *posted price* by 1947 had been increased, with many large companies resisting the advances, to around $2.50 per barrel for average-type crude. They finally had to pay, or lose their crude oil connections. They raised their *posted prices* each time, only when the payment of premiums had become so widespread that the existing *posted price* had become little more than a fiction.

37

This period saw several examples of a so-called "two-price" situation. Various companies took the initiative in the successive mark-ups of crude oil from around $1.20 in 1945 to around $2.50 in 1947. And so, on occasions, there was a tussle of opinion in which one company would raise its *posted price,* and perhaps be followed by a second, but others, however, would not follow.

In such cases, the industry held its breath to see who would be right. Millions of dollars were involved. If the higher price was a correct estimate of the outlook, the companies stubbornly sticking to the lower price would lose oil connections at one end of their business and so be unable to supply customers at the other end. But if it was wrong, they would save money on their crude supplies and so be able to undersell their competitors. The higher prices won until 1947. In the fall of 1948 two well-known companies made a sharp increase in their *posted prices.* Other companies did not follow. Again the trade waited to see. Then a turn took place in the demand—downward; and the two companies moved their *posted price* back in line with the rest of the industry. Since 1947 there has been no further general increase in crude oil prices to this time. (January 1953)

c. CRUDE PRICES AND WILDCATTING

There is a general feeling among oil men that the level of crude oil prices has a strong influence on the country's future supply of oil. The assumption is that the higher the price of crude oil, the more the incentive for individuals and companies to risk money on exploration and drilling. And the number of new wells drilled has a quite close correlation with the amount of new oil found. An analogy is drawn with the home-and-apartment-building industry, where rising rents encourage building and lower rents discourage it.

Too many of what statisticians call variables affect oil drilling to make this a "statistically verified principle." Too many things keep changing at the same time for the statisticians' comfort. Among the variables is technology. There have been rapid advances in geophysics and the techniques of drilling in the last three or four years. These may have lowered the cost of *wildcatting,* (drilling in unproved territory) in relation to the price of the crude oil which is the reward of *wildcatting* success. This might explain, for instance, why drilling has continued to increase in recent years although the crude oil price-level is virtually unchanged since 1947.

But it remains obvious that the price of crude must be an important influence on exploration and *wildcat* drilling. If the price of crude were cut in half, these would certainly lag, and if it were doubled they would certainly increase sharply; and if the statisticians' ideal of "other things being equal" were ever reached in the ever-changing oil industry, smaller changes would certainly have an ultimate effect on the rate of increase in the nation's proved reserves of crude.

D. CONSERVATION AND PRICES

In the old days when an oil field was discovered, everybody rushed to get the oil out fast. Men ravished new oil fields as a bear plunders wild honey. Wells sunk by the hundreds within a few feet of each other flowed the oil until it glutted pipe lines and markets, exhausting pressures and wasting irreplaceable underground reserves. In consequence oil prices dropped to absurd levels as the country had more oil than it could handle, then rose as oil grew scarce again.

For in those early days little was known about the nature of oil in the ground and there were no conservation laws to govern oil production. Each man was entitled to get what he could out of any wells he could drill on his land; and if he didn't get it himself, his neighbor would.

These wasteful methods have long since been curbed. Oil men have spent millions of dollars to advance the science of oil conservation, and have learned how to make sure they get all the oil possible from every field, without waste. Under the laws of most oil-producing states, wells must now be properly spaced and evenly flowed. Engineers have figured the *maximum efficient recovery* rate at which the oil of each field can be flowed and state laws hold back any faster flow.

The result has been (1) a vast extension of the life of the nation's oil reserves; (2) the saving of billions of barrels of oil otherwise lost; and (3) a steadying of the rate of oil production between the extremes of glut and scarcity. This has saved the country billions of barrels of oil and thereby saved consumers billions of dollars.

It also helped in World War II. The industry might not have done so well then if it hadn't learned not to blow its top every time it found a new oil field.

MARKET DEMAND

The authorities of several states now restrain the flowing of oil in excess of estimated market demand. These estimates come in part from the U. S. Bureau of Mines, in part from the *nominations* of crude oil buyers. The restrictions are enforced under state laws.

Some critics of the oil industry have claimed that these state restrictions on allowable oil production have held up the price of crude oil and of refined products. There are several reasons for doubting this, certainly over the long run.

1. The allowables are based on careful estimates of prospective consumption and demand. They have not prevented production from rising rapidly in the last two years so that an over 20 per cent increase in consumption has not resulted in any increase in petroleum prices even while the general price level was rising sharply.

2. Nor have they encouraged either buyers or state authorities to restrict production for the sake of pushing up prices. Such action would be a form of slow economic suicide, since any buyer holding down its *nominations* for crude, or any state holding down its own citizens' allowable production for the purpose of pushing up prices, would soon be replaced by others in the market—a possibility that has repeatedly been aired by some of the parties to the arrangement.

3. The only plausible complaint against the arrangement from the consumer's viewpoint, might be that at times it has prevented a flood of unwanted crude oil from coming on the market and driving prices down to his temporary advantage. But it is highly doubtful that the consumer's long-run interest would have been thus furthered. The oil thus so far prevented from coming on the market is now available in the form of reserves, and will be released whenever future demand calls for it.

CHAPTER VI

FORTY YEARS OF HARD COMPETITION [1]

Probably some people outside the so-called oil country still think of the oil industry in terms of the old STANDARD OIL combine and Ida Tarbell's "History of the Standard Oil Trust."

But that history is about as true of the oil industry today as "Uncle Tom's Cabin" is of the present-day South. In fact, some oil industry old-timers say that the Tarbell history, which set many people against the oil industry, wasn't much more of a true picture of the pre-1911 oil industry than Harriet Stowe's book was of the ante-bellum South.

A. THREE DEVELOPMENTS AROUND 1911

The modern history of the American oil industry starts around 1911. About that time the nation saw three major developments affecting oil. They raised the curtain on one of the greatest competitive developments in all industrial history. They were: (1) The development of the low-priced automobile; (2) The discovery and rapid development of shallow fields of sweet, easily refined crude oil of high gasoline content in the middle of the United States; and (3) The break-up of the old STANDARD OIL combine in 1911.

Break-up of the Combine

The old STANDARD OIL COMPANY, by order of the United States Supreme Court in 1911, was broken up into 34 independent parts—23 oil companies and 11 pipelines. The old STANDARD OIL COMPANY continued as the present STANDARD OIL COMPANY (N. J.), incorporated in New Jersey. Thirty-three oil and pipeline companies were split off from it. The severed companies were forbidden by the Supreme Court to ever unite again except with court permission, and in only one case of any consequence have slivers of the old combine ever come together again.[2]

---

[1] Much of the material in this chapter is adapted from articles in the March 9, 1949 issue of NATIONAL PETROLEUM NEWS.

[2] Standard Oil Company of New York, doing chiefly a gasoline business, was allowed by federal court in the early 'thirties to merge with Vacuum Oil Company, specializing in lubricants. Other combinations of successor Standard companies since 1911 include the following: Solar Refining Company was bought out by Standard Oil Company of Ohio in 1931. Standard Oil Company of Nebraska was consolidated into Standard Oil Company of Indiana in 1939. Standard Oil Company of Indiana acquired the assets of the Standard Oil Company of Kansas in 1932. The Indiana Pipeline Company was merged with the Buckeye Pipeline Company. The New York Transit Company and Northern Pipeline Companies were owned by the Buckeye Pipeline Company.

Today the competition between former STANDARD companies is indistinguishable from the general competition in the oil companies. Former STANDARD companies compete in every state in the Union directly or through subsidiaries. In some states as many as six compete.

Gasoline Outgrows Kerosine

The evolution of the rich man's "touring car" into the popular "gas buggy" brought a rapid shift in the demand for petroleum products. Kerosine had been the industry's major product; in the old days gasoline had even occasionally been thrown away for lack of market. Now the demand for gasoline began to swell.

New Oil Discoveries

As if perhaps by lucky accident, a number of new oil fields were discovered, beginning with the Cushing, Oklahoma, field in 1912, which had an unusually high gasoline content. These fields were in the middle of the country; their oil was easily refined; and the new supply was in a volume no one had ever seen or heard of before.

The rush of circumstances was almost too much for the successors of the STANDARD combine. Their business grew, but not nearly as fast as the industry. Within a dozen years after the break-up the percentage of the country's total oil business handled by the ex-subsidiaries dropped from 85 per cent to 35 per cent. And historians have raised the question of whether, if the combine had not been broken up and the members had not been pushed into the cool stream of aggressive competition, the combine would not have fallen even farther behind in the race.

As new fields were discovered and exploited, and the industry expanded enormously, competition became more severe in all departments. It was severe in production, where lax rules allowed oil to be drawn out of the ground too fast, but where new discoveries were being made constantly. It was severe in refining, where it constantly encouraged new techniques, from distillation to modern cracking. It was severe in transportation, where owners of pipe lines, tankers, river-barges, product pipe lines, and ocean tankers, fought to see who could get there "firstest with the mostest," cheapest. It was severe in distribution, where many former small companies rose in national size and became considerably larger than many of the former STANDARD companies.

One of the leading forms of this competition was the expansion of many companies in one part of the business into others. This has come to be called integration. In 1911, there were hardly any integrated companies in the business. The old STANDARD companies were by no means fully integrated. They were chiefly refiners. They also had pipe lines, and they marketed. Only three were in production.

Since then, however, oil producers have gone into refining, refiners have gone into production, and distributors have gone into refining, as men in each branch of the industry have seen opportunities of cutting into other branches of the industry.

The word "integrated" is at best a relative term. No company today is in the complete sense of the phrase "fully integrated"—that is, producing all it transports, transporting all it refines, and refining all it distributes—or vice versa. Most of the so-called *majors* fall far short of this imagined total integration. None of them are self-sufficient "from drill to driveway."

B. ADVANCES IN PRODUCTION, REFINING, TRANSPORT AND DISTRIBUTION

Competition in the producing end resulted in the introduction of geologists in the decade ending 1920. In the oil fields, competitors began to get ahead of each other by the use of such devices as the seismograph, gravity meter, magnetometer, electric well logging, photogeology, micropaleontology, microstratigraphy, and radioactive well logging.

In refinery competition, after World War I the industry began to use research laboratories. During the 1920's it became common to hear that "Dr. So-and-So is head of the refinery operations." In the last ten years or so refiners have spent hundreds of millions on new cost-cutting and quality-raising investments such as: (1) new catalytic cracking processes yielding among other things higher octane and super aviation gasolines; (2) new ways of handling sour crudes once not good for refining; (3) new processes for making synthetic liquid fuels; and (4) the country's fast-growing new petrochemical industry.

In transportation, competitors brought in a great number of new lower-cost methods. First, great fleets of railroad tank-cars were put

43

in operation. Then there was developed a vast network of crude-oil pipe lines. Fleets of tankers moving from Gulf to Eastern seaboard were increased in total size and in economy of operation. Then competitors began using river barges. Next there came a growing use of the so-called transport truck carrying 5,000 gallons or more over the highways. Recently competitors have put in thousands of miles of so-called product pipe lines, through which the finished products from refineries are piped *out of* them as well as the crude oil that is piped *into* them. In oil transportation "everything changes except the element of change."

In distribution, competitors have over the years likewise put in one innovation after another. They began with the service station, the first of which was introduced around 1910. From there on for about 20 years the leading distributors built themselves chains of service stations. Then the *trackside operator* had his cost-cutting day.

Perhaps one of the most notable developments in distribution in the four decades has been the growth of independent oil jobbing. In 1911, neither the STANDARD companies nor the growing independents of the day sold through jobbers, but direct. Subsequent historians of the industry say that in those days there were only about 125 jobbers in the industry. Today there are an estimated 14,000.

These jobbers are usually considered as in the category of small business. Nevertheless their businesses generally run larger than that of the groceries, hardware stores and garages in their own towns, and their individual investment sometimes runs to several million dollars. And they have pioneered in such fields as home heating oils, and the recently developed liquefied petroleum gas (*LPG*). Yet, their independent existence is little known to the public, since many of them handle the widely-advertised brands of larger companies.

Developments in each of the above-mentioned branches of the industry have caused a more or less radical reorganization in the general direction of lower prices to the consumer, effected through hard competition.

C. "BATTLE OF THE FUELS"

As the oil industry grew larger, its competitive battles expanded externally and multiplied internally.

A giant three-cornered "battle of the fuels" developed in recent years between fuel oil, bituminous coal, and natural gas. Oil had already replaced soft coal in ships' bunkers as the world's leading ocean-going fuel for ships' boilers. Fuel oil began to encroach further on coal as the favorite fuel for power plants in factories, steel mills, and electric power stations. Many of these switched to fuel oil; others put in installations which would let them switch back and forth from oil to coal depending on the relative advantages of price, convenience, reliability, and so on. As this competition was developing, natural gas, a product of the search for oil, entered the competition and made it a triangle. Meantime, oil jobbers developed the use of home-heating oils to the point where they competed with anthracite.

But over and above its competition with bituminous coal and anthracite, the oil industry has developed competition within itself among its own divisions.

Thus sellers of diesel oil compete not only in the railroad market with soft-coal companies but also with sellers of gasoline to highway truck users. In fact, a three-cornered competition has developed in engine-fuels between gasoline, diesel oil, and liquefied petroleum gas (*LPG*) with the latter making competitive inroads on the bus and farm market—in some limited areas. *LPG* is now also proving a strong competitor in the home-heating market, creating still another competitive quadrangle—coal, heating-oil, natural gas and *LPG*.

CHAPTER VII

"PROOF OF THE PUDDING"

A. WHAT PRICE GASOLINE TODAY

Gasoline is still the principal product of the oil industry. It comes to about 42 per cent of the output. It also has a nearly two per cent weight in the consumers' price index of the Bureau of Labor Statistics, which is based on consumers' buying habits in medium-sized cities.

So it is chosen here as "proof of the pudding," price-wise, of what the oil industry's competition has produced. Other petroleum product prices would show nearly the same story, by comparison with average wholesale prices and with the cost of living.

Not counting state and federal taxes, the average retail price of gasoline today is about the same as it was 25 years ago.

Gone is the nickel cigar, the dollar watch, the five-cent cup of coffee, the "jitney" ride, and even in some cities the nickel phone call. But the driving public still gets its gasoline for the same price before tax as in 1925.

> In the summer of 1925, an average motorist, driving into an average station, in an average city in the United States, would have seen on the gasoline pump: "PRICE 21.93 cents, TAX 2.28 cents, TOTAL 24.21 cents."
>
> But on December 1, 1951, driving into the same average station in the same average city, he would have seen something like: "PRICE 20.31 cents, TAX 7.32 cents, TOTAL 27.63 cents."
>
> The wholesale price of gasoline has done even better. It is perceptibly lower than a quarter-century ago. Regular-grade gasoline in cargo lots at Gulf Coast refineries sold in mid-1951 at around 11 cents a gallon. In mid-1925 it sold at around 14¼ cents.

Some other basic prices have moved meantime as follows:

	1925	1951
Gold (ounce)	$20.67	$35.00
Corn (bushel)	.70	1.80
Iron (gross ton, Foundry No. 2, Pittsburgh)	21.64	52.50
Cotton (lb.)	.20	.40
Copper (lb.)	.13	.24½

46

B. WHAT GASOLINE? QUALITY IMPROVEMENTS

But today's is not the same as yesterday's motor-fuel. *Gasoline* is not just *gasoline*. What the motorist buys today for the same ex-tax price as 25 years ago is a far superior engine-fuel to the gasoline he or his father bought then.

Everybody realizes how much more value per pound there is in the modern automobile than in the car of a quarter-century ago. They can see it and feel it. But few people realize that modern gasoline has been similarly improved; for gasoline today looks and smells about the same as it did 25 years ago. Yet it has been engineered and improved in a host of ways.

Nowadays many motorists buy their gasoline in part on the basis of octane ratings. Today's *regular* branded gasolines average something around 83.7 octane and today's *premium* gasolines something around 91.

But, as a comparison, it may be of interest that the gasoline with which Lindbergh's "Spirit of St. Louis" was fueled on the first eastbound crossing of the Atlantic in 1927, had an octane rating of, by present standards, only 73. And that was presumably as good *premium* gasoline as was then obtainable.

So rapid has been the advance in this characteristic alone of gasoline that it has been difficult for engineers and research workers to make accurate comparisons between the gasoline of today and that of 1925. Few people outside of laboratories at that time had even heard of octanes or knew about anti-knock ratings. Students of oil history have had to get the engineers in some cases actually to reconstruct the earlier refining processes from the oil books, since there is no 1925 gasoline still standing around, and then to make extensive calculations, to discover the comparable ratings.

As best the engineers can establish, the average 1925 *regular* gasoline rated about a 55 octane number. And the *premium* gasoline of 1925, sold then in an insignificant number of stations, rated 71 octane. Such gasoline used in any modern car would almost make the engine knock standing still.

But octane ratings are only one measure of the ways in which gasolines have been improved. The gum content and the amount of corrosive agents have been greatly reduced, so that engines do not carbon up or wear out the way they used to. Modern branded gasolines are tailored for quick starting in winter in cold sections of the country by the addition of butane, and for correct vaporization, and against vapor-lock, in the summer and in warm regions of the country. "Quality competition" has led competing oil companies to make improvement after improvement in their gasoline. Like cooks, oil companies have tried to set out better dishes in the hope that what might be called the gourmets among drivers would pick the most desirable product even without knowing or asking how the better job was done, the better gasoline produced, or the better performance obtained.

c. LOWERED COST OF GASOLINE "PERFORMANCE"

Many different kinds of engineering tests have shown that today's gasoline has been improved at least 50 per cent in the past 25 years— or in other words that it takes only about two gallons of today's gasoline to do what took three gallons in 1925. For example:

> The useful power of automobile engines has been increased by about 50 per cent.

> The miles per gallon delivered by gasoline "under conditions of comparable performance" have been increased by about 50 per cent.

> The performance of typical automobiles, measured by acceleration time to given speeds, has been increased more than 50 pr cent.

> The time required to warm up an engine has been cut about in half; and unsatisfactory performance and actual stalling of cars from gasoline gum troubles has decreased almost to zero.

Hence, today, from two gallons of gasoline, costing about 42 cents before taxes, today's motorist can get about as much as his father could get in 1925, from three gallons costing about 66 cents before taxes.

Meantime, the average of other things like food, clothing, housing, and so on, that cost him or his father about 66 cents in 1925, now cost around $1.00.

So the (1925) 66 cents worth of other things now costs around a dollar; but the (1925) 66 cents worth of gasoline performance now costs around 42 cents before taxes.

Of course the taxes have gone up on other things too. But even if today's prices on these other things are adjusted for tax increases, it is evident that in terms of these other things, the cost of a given amount of gasoline *performance* has been cut *at least in half*.

(Credit is due here also to the automobile industry. It developed the engines that could use the better fuels efficiently.)

D. WHO GAINS?

The private motorist is not the only beneficiary of this price-and-quality competition in the oil industry. Higher octanes and compression ratios have enabled the designers of trucks and buses to increase the pay-load ton-miles of trucks per gallon of gasoline consumed, and the average speed of inter-city buses, by about 50 per cent. And the farmer on today's tractor can pull three plows while on the latest 1925 tractor he could pull only two.

This has contributed to a great change.

In 1925, city people depended on an extensive system of street-car lines. The great bulk of the nation's freight moved by rail. And most farmers depended on horses.

Today the motor-bus has largely supplanted the street-car, and in some cases even the "steam-cars." Millions of motor trucks move almost every form of freight. And cash-crop farmers use tractors almost entirely instead of horses.

Oil industry competition in price and quality has been largely responsible. Today, a gallon of gasoline weighing around 6½ pounds usually costs about four cents a pound and one of those four cents goes to the tax collector. Even with the increased taxes it would be hard to find a bigger bargain among all the things that Americans eat, wear, or use.

CHAPTER VIII

FROM THEORY TO PRACTICE

Professional critics of American industry have a number of theoretical criticisms of the way prices are made. Three of their favorite criticisms have been frequently levelled against the oil industry. They are that:

1. Often everybody quotes the same price. And sameness or uniformity of prices supposedly means collusion or conspiracy.

2. Often price changes are initiated by "dominant" companies, sometimes called "price leaders." And this leadership supposedly means that these companies have too much power.

3. Often strong companies are supposed to have enough economic power to ignore some of the full force of "pure competition." Instead, it is charged, their "concentration of economic power" permits them to avoid competition and to rely instead on "administered prices."

A. IDENTICAL PRICES

"CONSCIOUS PARALLEL ACTION"

People who drive down a highway and see the same price posted at every service station for some miles, down to the decimal point, sometimes feel that "it's all a conspiracy."

They have powerful company in this uninformed reaction. The Federal Trade Commission in Washington, in a press release in the summer of 1948, said:

"The Commission chose to rely on the obvious fact that the economic effect of identical prices, achieved through *conscious parallel action,* is the same as that of similar prices achieved through overt collusion; and for this reason the Commission treated the *conscious parallelism of action* as a violation of the Federal Trade Commission Act."

What the FTC meant by this heavy language was that when competitors know they charge the same price, they get the same result as if they got together and conspired.

This could make it illegal for anyone to charge the same price as his competitor's if he is *conscious* that his price is *parallel* to his competitor's. In fact if this view prevailed it could mean that an automobile driver who said to a service station operator, "Look across the street; your competitor is charging only 27 cents a gallon so give me the same price," would be urging the dealer toward an illegal conscious parallel action.

OFF-PRICE AND NON-PRICE COMPETITION

Oil product prices, in point of fact, vary commonly from one seller to another. The reader who doubts it is invited to spend an hour driving around from one gasoline service station to another checking prices. In any twenty stations within a mile radius from a given point in a populous area he will find a wide variation even in the *posted price*.

If he checks more carefully he will learn of *behind-the-pump* and *under-the-canopy* concessions. And if he makes one more check, as to the variations in service, courtesy, and convenience offered, he will find differences enough to make it fairly easy for him to pick which station he would rather continue dealing with.

And if he made the same kind of survey in the wholesale oil-product business he would find the same general fact. Though buying oil products is not quite like buying rugs in Bagdad it still has a faint tinge of horse-trading.

Off-price and non-price competition (quality, service, location, reputability, etc.) are characteristic of the oil industry from retailing clear back to the sale and purchase of crude oil. As an oil man has said, "No two competitors in any market ever offer the customer quite the same inducements. Each very properly appeals to his customer in keeping with his character and personality, or that of his firm."

COMPETITION TENDS TOWARD UNIFORMITY

Yet, the normal trend in competition is toward uniformity of product and of prices. The more competitive markets are found where everybody is offering standard goods at standard prices with standard discounts or premiums for quality, location, and so on.

Nor does identity of price, policy, or action by itself prove collusion. When Russia and the United States both develop jet planes and atom bombs, they are not necessarily acting in collusion or conspiracy.

Recently, Charles Sawyer, then Secretary of Commerce, remarked:

> "Mere similarity or so-called 'parallelism' of action . . . is likely in a normal competitive situation, to result from informed competition. Similar conditions result in similar action if there is adequate knowledge. When supply is adequate, prices and terms on standard goods tend to be uniform at any given moment at the level most favorable to the buyer. There is no reason, therefore, to condemn mere parallelism of action as indicating a lack of effective competition."[1]

A prominent group of New York lawyers recently wrote:

> "From our observation there is no contention that creates greater uncertainty and sense of helpless insecurity among businessmen than that 'conscious similarity' (of pricing) is in itself unlawful."[2]

An ironic comment on the criticism of uniform prices was recently made by a former chairman of the Federal Trade Commission. Speaking before a group of sales executives and purchasing agents he said:

> "Be sure you don't know your competitors' prices. . . . This is difficult. What happens when one of your salesmen walks into a store and offers a retailer one of your 1948 models of rubber-mounted shaving mugs at $13.75 the dozen?

> "The first thing the purchasing agent says is, 'Why you poor so-and-so, Glutz is selling his mugs for $12.95.'

> "This means the jig is up. For . . . if you come down to $12.95, you are matching competitors' prices, and that . . . if carried out systematically, results in a conscious parallelism of action which . . . is tantamount to a conspiracy.

> "There is, however, a way of getting around this difficulty. Equip all your salesmen with earmuffs . . . my apparent flippancy is but the cry of a man who sees in these cases the seed of internal decay for our distribution system . . ."[3]

SHOULD EVERYBODY QUOTE LOWER THAN EVERYBODY ELSE ?

It would sometimes seem that those who look askance at identical prices really would like to see everybody selling lower than everybody

---

[1] Address, 20th National Business Conference, Harvard Business School Association, Boston, June 10, 1950.
[2] Memorandum for the President's Committee on Business and Government Relations, submitted by a Special Committee of the Section on Antitrust Law of the New York State Bar Association, July 10, 1950.
[3] Remarks of Lowell B. Mason, Boston Conference on Distribution, October 26, 1948.

else. Oil men sometimes feel that this is almost the way prices are actually made in their industry.

B. PRICE INITIATIVE

Many people misunderstand the thing called *price leadership* in the oil industry. They think that oil prices are *set* by the predominant companies in different areas and then followed by everyone else.

As these people see it, when oil men follow-the-leader on prices, this seems to give the predominant companies in any particular part of the business a great and dangerous power either to raise prices against the public or to lower them against competitors.

Since somebody always has to take the initiative in price-changes, let us see how these changes generally occur.

GUESSING WITH A BIG STAKE

To begin with, the sales managers of all companies competing in a given territory, whether large or small, keep constant watch on all the factors which should affect price. These include general economic conditions, fluctuations in their own sales volume, the tactics of their competitors, and so on.

A downtrend may be foreshadowed in a number of ways. It may be indicated of course by persistent price wars in certain areas. It may be indicated if the company's salesmen come in with reports from customers that competitors are making concessions, giving discounts, or cutting prices quietly.

The sales manager of every company must make his own guess as to what is causing these things. He must figure whether they are due to fundamental causes or to merely transient influences. They may result from a decline in costs, particularly the wholesale cost of the product, or perhaps from lower transport or distribution costs. Or they may indicate that a powerful competitor is trying to break into the market. But the sales manager's chief problem is to decide whether they are signs of a fundamental trend or of some temporary influence on the market.

ON THE DOWNSIDE

The company with the largest volume of business, of course, has the largest stake in finding the correct answer. For if the trend is really down and the company does not go along, its price-cutting competitors will soon be joyfully taking away its customers—and it has more customers to lose than anybody else in the area. But if the trend is merely a passing one, and the fundamental market situation is sound, yet it nevertheless cuts, it will not only lose in profits but it may also inspire charges by its smaller competitors that it is driving them out of business—*monopoly*.

So, the largest marketer in an area seldom leads the market down. In a declining market he is more often a *price follower* than a *price leader*.

Some people think that leading marketers occasionally reduce prices to drive out competition so that they may later enjoy a monopoly. But, as one oil man has put it, "That is like trying to sweep back the ocean to get a dry place to sit down." Competition is impelled by impersonal forces that never scare, and never hesitate for long, and would move in immediately when prices were restored, offering little opportunity to a single marketer to recoup his losses.

An amusing angle of the competitive story on oil is that sometimes companies considered pillars of price respectability in their customary market areas decide to expand, and so become *enfants terribles* or troublesome price influences in other companies' customary markets. Long ago the fledgling independent STANDARD companies, for instance, began invading each others' once sacrosanct markets. Today a west-coast company is invading the Atlantic seaboard market, some eastern companies are invading mid-west markets, and in general no sales division manager in the oil business can afford to take the afternoon off for golf too often.

ON THE UPSIDE

During the 1930's, the trend of petroleum product prices was largely downward. During the 1940's, however, it was slowly upward. But when the marketing fundamentals point upward the problem of the leading marketer in any product or area is quite different.

The signals for a price advance in petroleum products may be of various sorts, such as higher crude prices, higher refinery prices, larger distribution costs, a heavier demand on the part of the public, and the appearance of scarcities and shortages here and there.

But few smaller marketers will dare to take the initiative and raise prices if the biggest marketer in the area hasn't moved. They run too large a risk of losing business to him.

On the other hand, the largest marketer also runs his own risks in advancing his prices. He has the largest stake of all in guessing right. He can only guess whether his competitors will follow his advance or will seize on his mis-calculation to move in on his customers. If competitors don't follow, and he has mis-calculated, confusion will result and he will eventually have to retreat.

WHO WANTS TO LEAD?

To be continuously successful in taking the initiative in price changes, a sales manager or company must continuously use superior judgment in appraising trends. Unless a company which is the so-called leading marketer in an area accurately interprets basic forces and local conditions, it soon will not be the *price leader* and the initiative will shift to somebody else. Success in price initiative is not the reward of size; but size is sometimes the reward of repeated success in price initiative.

And, as with heavy-weight champions, the lot of the executives of the leading marketer in an area is not a happy one. They must keep on guessing right on prices. If they guess wrong on the downside they lose more profits than anybody else and if they guess wrong on the upside they lose more business than anybody else. And since the *price leader* is usually the first to raise prices and not the first to reduce them, there is always a period after the raise and before the reduction when his competitors are nibbling away at his business.

In recent years and with increasing frequency, companies other than the leading marketer have initiated price changes themselves. In all branches of the industry, oil men are familiar with these shifts of price initiative.

These are contests of judgment; but though the outcome appears only in slow motion, like that of a chess-game, they have nevertheless been dramatic. The prize of success on the upside is more profit and on the downside more volume; the penalty of misjudgment on the upside is loss of volume and on the downside loss of profit. Often millions of dollars are at stake.

For instance in the middle of 1947, one of the largest marketers in the New York and New England area thought it saw a strong basic price situation, and announced a general price advance. But the largest marketer in that area viewed the outlook differently and did not meet the advance. More important, neither did other competitors. Two days later the advance was rescinded—and just in time. Subsequent trends showed that it was unsound.

Another such miscalculation already mentioned occurred in crude oil prices in the fall of 1948. A medium-sized major oil company raised its posted price for crude oil by 35 cents. It was followed by one other company of about the same size and by a few smaller companies. The rest of the industry did not go along. Within a few weeks the increase was rescinded.

On the other hand more than half of the price advances made in the East in the last year or so were initiated by companies not at the time considered as the market-leaders in the particular area for the particular product involved.

PRICE INITIATIVE IS NOT PRICE CONTROL

In general, people who have mistaken price *initiative* for price *control* have probably paid too much attention to posted, listed, and otherwise published prices. These prices, though highly useful to oil men for reference purposes, fall far short of indicating the almost infinite variety, continual change, and pervading competition which characterizes oil prices.

Price leadership in the oil industry is somewhat like the possession of initiative in an informal group of boys. The leader is not elected, nor does he hold office for any particular term. He lasts as a leader only so long as he keeps guessing right on the trend.

As an oil man said to the Temporary National Economic Committee:

"In summary . . . so-called price leadership in the petroleum industry boils down to the fact that some company in each territory most of the time bears the onus of formally recognizing current conditions

... (But) unless the so-called price leader accurately interprets basic conditions and local conditions, it soon will not be the leading marketer. Price leadership does not mean that the price leader can set prices to get the maximum profit and force other marketers to conform . . ."[1]

This kind of initiative is not peculiar to the oil industry. It is found in many other industries where there is large-scale production of standardized commodities like steel, cement, sugar, non-ferrous metals, textiles, etc., and even in many manufacturing industries like those which produce automobiles, farm machinery, tires, and so on, where successful price-making involves the calculation of a multitude of long-term market influences.

C. FIRM PRICES

Critics level another charge against the way oil prices are made. They use as a yardstick what they call *a perfectly competitive market* or *pure competition.* In such a market, they feel that no seller would have any discretion as to the price he would receive and no choice but to take what he could get or stay out of the market. This would be because he would be only a very small and unimpressive factor in such a market, like a small independent refiner, presumably with distress gasoline to sell at one time, though at another time able to ask a very good price indeed.   .

The ideal market which these critics seem to have in mind would be something like the stock or commodity exchanges, where no buyer or seller is really big enough to influence the market, where the market is primarily made by unknown or automatic forces, and where bids and offers are normally made at the market.

The critics assume that people who can set their prices for some time on a take-it-or-leave-it basis, are more than likely to use this power to hold prices up. These critics seem suspicious of all price-making which is not an impromptu reaction to what the Victorian economists called the "higgling of the market." They call these steady quotations *administered prices*—a term of opprobrium in certain economists' circles despite its deadpan use.

[1] TNEC Hearings, Part 15, p. 8702.

Yet such firm prices, set for some time on the basis of careful calculations, have long been a part of the nation's price system, and they do not indicate any lack of competition. Motor-car manufacturers set their list prices even before they offer their cars. Steel prices stay steady for months. Price lists are published by many industries. Mail order houses issue catalogs with prices and abide by them; department stores put price-tags on their goods instead of leaving it to their clerks to haggle like an Oriental shop-keeper with each new customer.

Likewise, oil men figure their prices several moves ahead where they can. Even the retail gasoline dealer, small though his share of the total business, makes his calculations, figures what price to charge, and does not change it unless he is convinced it does not fit the market. In the wholesale gasoline market a large part of the business is done on long-term contract. Oil prices are as often studied guesses on the future as they are impromptu reactions to the present.

One of the factors which oil men weigh most heavily in arriving at their quoting prices is cost.

The relations between cost and market price have long been studied by economists. The immediate determinant of prices is usually supply and demand; but the ultimate determinant is cost. As every boy knows who ever sold lemonade at a fair, the weather may make his product worth ten cents a glass, or nothing at all; but if the fair lasts long enough and he has several competitors, and he wants to fix a price for some time, he will have to make a price which bears some relation to what Mother paid for the sugar and the lemons.

In the oil industry many operations, like the construction of modern refineries costing 10 to 100 million dollars, take years to pay out, and directors called upon to approve such expenditures must look beyond what they may consider to be merely temporary high- or low-price situations.

Nor are such long-range considerations the exclusive worry of the Mr. Bigs in the industry. Where they debate over spending a million, a jobber may have to think over spending a hundred thousand and a retailer over spending a thousand dollars.

CHAPTER IX

CONCLUSION

A. YARDSTICKS OF COMPETITION

Since some people now criticize the way the oil industry makes its prices, yet urge the desirability of competition, it is worth while to measure the industry by some yardsticks as to the degree of its competition.

By two of the most obvious methods of appraisal, the industry deserves a good rating.

1. It is under constant criticism both for prices too high, and for prices too low. It can hardly be wrong on both counts.

2. It has a remarkably good price record. In fact, painful as it may sound inside the industry, an extra credit should be given it, from the consumer's viewpoint, for the sporadic price-wars in the industry's retail division.

But consumers' interest are today no longer the sole yardstick of an industry's competition. Some new gauges, in the minds of the courts and the public, are the following.

FREEDOM OF ENTRY

To serve the nation adequately, and to meet the exacting tests which politicians and the public now make, an industry cannot qualify as one with healthy competition unless it is reasonably easy for newcomers to enter.

In oil production the hard fact is that anybody is free to "lose his shirt" looking for oil. The "ante" averages between $50,000 and $500,000 per exploratory well and it takes about nine such wells on the average to hit oil. Still, people keep trying it.

But if this is a high entrance fee, its height is not due to any structural defects in the oil industry but merely to the fact that the industry has apparently exploited most of the shallower and less costly prospects of oil-bearing sands.

In transportaton, such as by pipe line and tanker, and in refining, the entrance fee is considerably higher. Pipe lines, for instance, cost from $20,000 to $100,000 a mile, new super-tankers up to $7,000,000 apiece, and the smallest refineries many millions.

> However, this is not necessarily big money for companies in one part of the business to put up to expand into some other part as they have been doing for forty years.

A man can of course go into distribution with considerably less capital. And the retail field is easiest to get into, particularly since it is almost always possible for a would-be dealer to get financial assistance, with or without the aid of a large supplier, to build a service station.

One thing that makes the oil industry comparatively easy to get into is the speed with which it keeps changing. In production, old fields run down and new fields have to be found. In refining, new techniques are constantly being developed. In transport and distribution, new methods offer repeated opportunities to ambitious would-be entrants.

RATE OF INNOVATION

Another obvious yardstick of how competitive an industry is, can be seen in how rapidly it develops new methods and processes.

By this yardstick the oil industry has hardly a peer. New techniques are constantly being introduced in all its four major branches—production, refining, transportation and distribution. It employs, for instance, about 15,000 people in its research laboratories, and spends well over $100,000,000 a year on research.

It has been said, in fact, that innovation is today the only true source of profits—and continuous innovation the only reliable source of continuous profits. Whether or not this is true, oil men act as though it were.

RATE AT WHICH BENEFITS OF INNOVATION REACH THE CONSUMER

It would not speak well for an industry if it kept the benefit of its technological advances largely to itself; that is, if for instance it offered its quality improvements only at higher prices, or it kept its technological cost reductions only as increased profits. But in the oil industry these, on the record, are quickly converted into better products for the same price or lower prices for the same product. Another way to measure this is in the rate of obsolescence which is the converse of the rate of technological advance as handed on to customers. This is hard to measure; but the rate is certainly high in oil.

B. ERRONEOUS YARDSTICKS OF COMPETITION

A number of yardsticks have been used to measure the degree of competition in oil and other industries which actually are not good yardsticks at all. These include the industry's degree of concentration, uniformity of prices, price leadership by the largest company, and earnings. These measures give no clue whatever to how competitive an industry may be.

1. Concentration. An industry may include only a few companies, yet be fiercely competitive. Only four or five companies dominate the television set business but no one would say that it is not highly competitive. Only a dozen companies make automobiles yet most people would consider this industry more competitive in the last two decades than the home-building industry which includes tens of thousands of financially unrelated contractors. If 48 companies each operated in one of the 48 states there would be less competition than if three companies each operated in every state. Furthermore there is hardly an industry whose products do not compete with those of other industries.

2. Uniformity of Prices. As indicated above, uniform prices may be and usually are the outward evidence of a competitive "cold war," not of collusion.

3. Price Leadership. As also indicated above, anybody's leadership in the changing of prices is no more than a result of his superior judgment, and fails if his judgment fails.

4. Earnings. High earnings are sometimes considered to indicate that an industry is not competing hard enough. But the opposite is more often the case; the most aggressive industries often show the highest earnings, and the most sluggish industries the lowest.

OIL INDUSTRY IN THE MIDDLE

By any of these futile yardsticks, however, the oil industry puts in a mediocre performance for better or for worse. It is about half-way down the list by any of these measures. It is much less concentrated than many other industries, since its largest company does only a ninth of the business and the critics of "Big Three's" and "Big Four's" of other industries have had to switch to a "Big Twenty" in oil. Its prices are far from uniform, and its largest companies are more often *price followers* than *price leaders*. And its earnings, which largely go back into new wells, refineries, and other plants, are about half-way down the list of industries whether compared to investment or to sales.

c. SOME QUESTIONS FOR FUTURE INVESTIGATORS

Two questions interest oil men. The first is whether competition in the oil industry is today more strenuous than it was forty years ago, or in the 'twenties or the 'thirties. Some say "yes" and some say "no." Of course, it is usually the younger men who say "yes."

The other question is how it happens that the oil industry has stayed so consistently competitive. One explanation is that it has always been too large and sprawling to be controlled, at least for the last forty years. Another explanation is that oil men have had too much frontier in their blood to yield to government controls except, as in World War II, when they had an even more serious war to fight than their customary competitive war.

Still another explanation is that the industry got started in such a way that its members developed a large vested interest in having the business free of vested interests.

There is room for a good historian to appraise these various explanations of why the American oil industry continues to be one of the most competitive businesses ever seen in all history on the whole face of the earth.